This book belongs to:

Color With Me!

Grandpa & Me Coloring Book Marine Life

Mary Lou Brown & Sandy Mahony

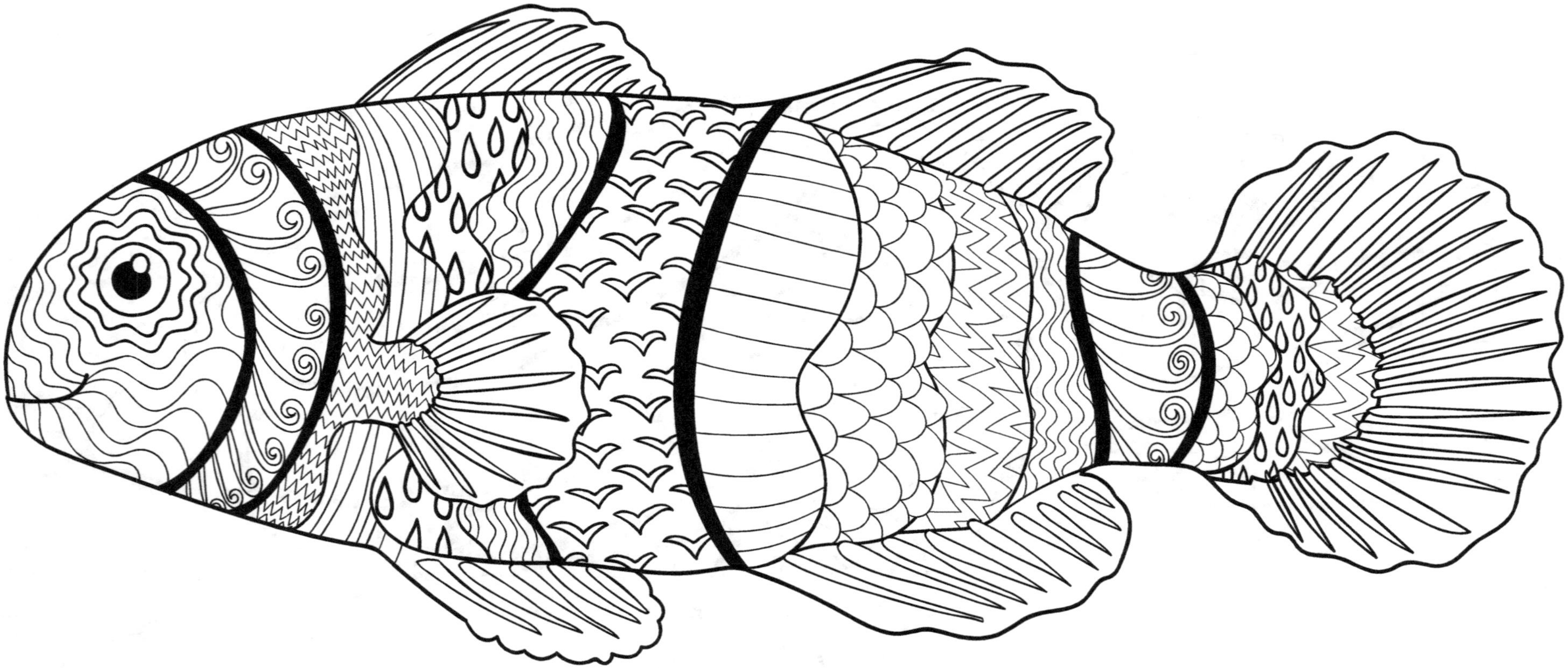

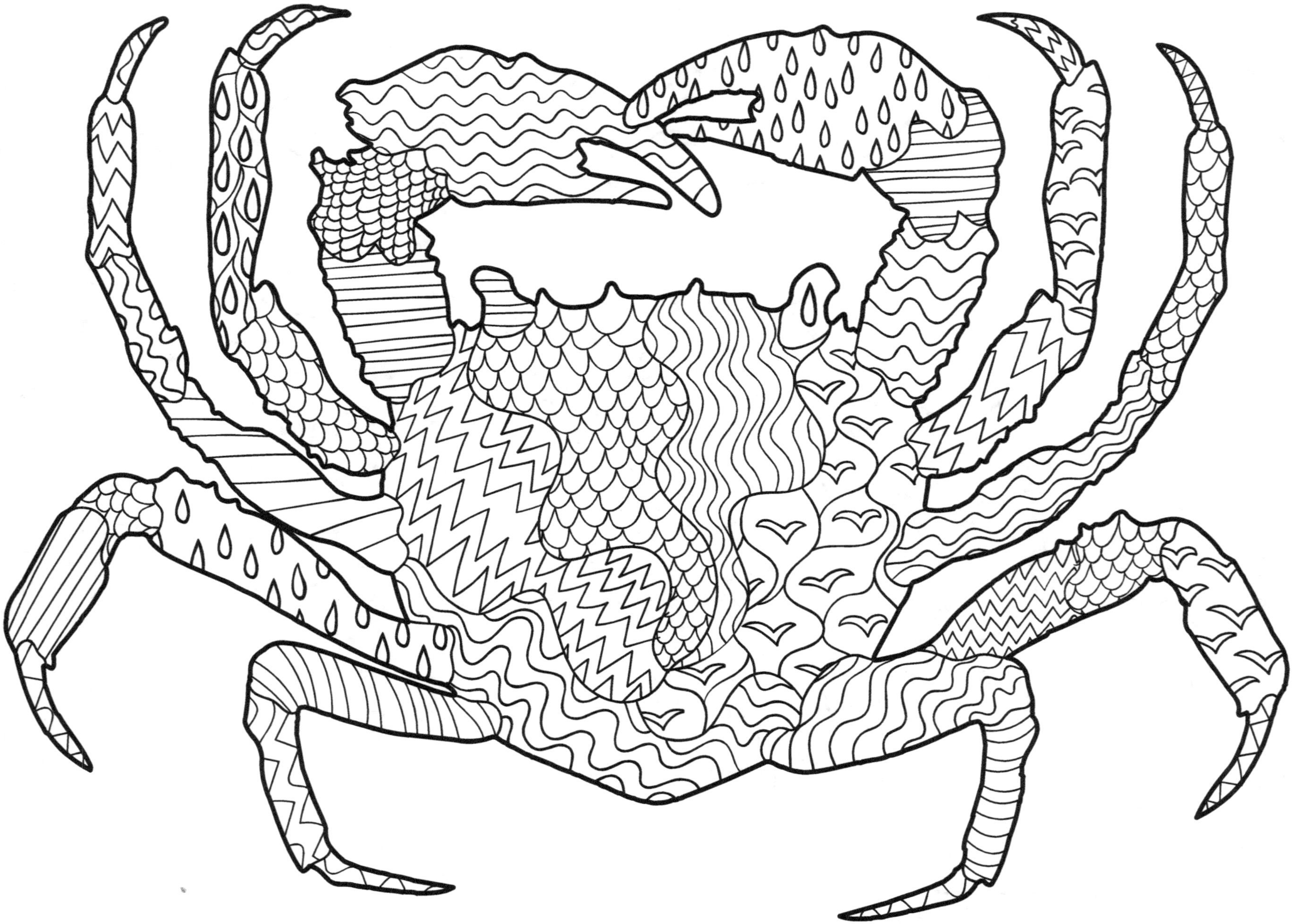

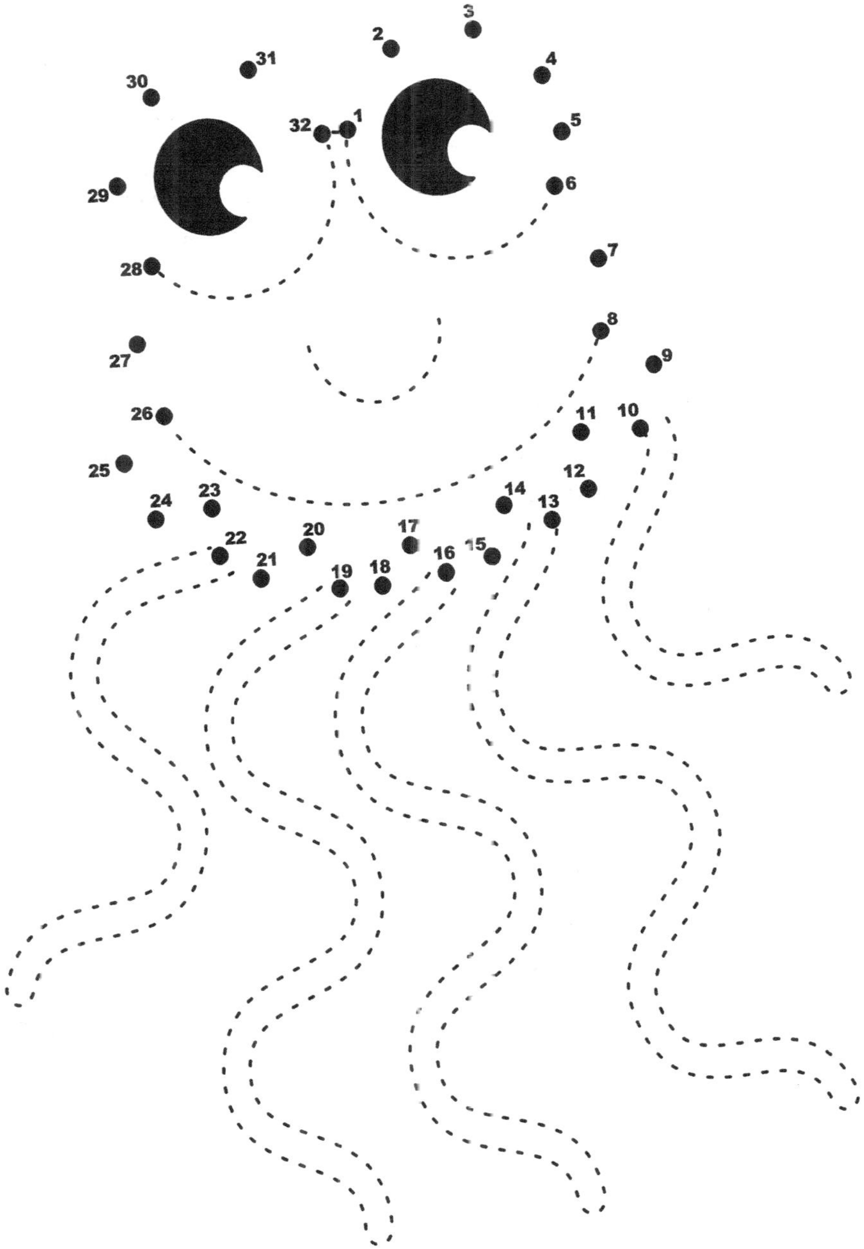
1
2
3
4
5
6
7
8
9
10
11
12
13
14
15
16
17
18
19
20
21
22
23
24
25
26
27
28
29
30
31
32

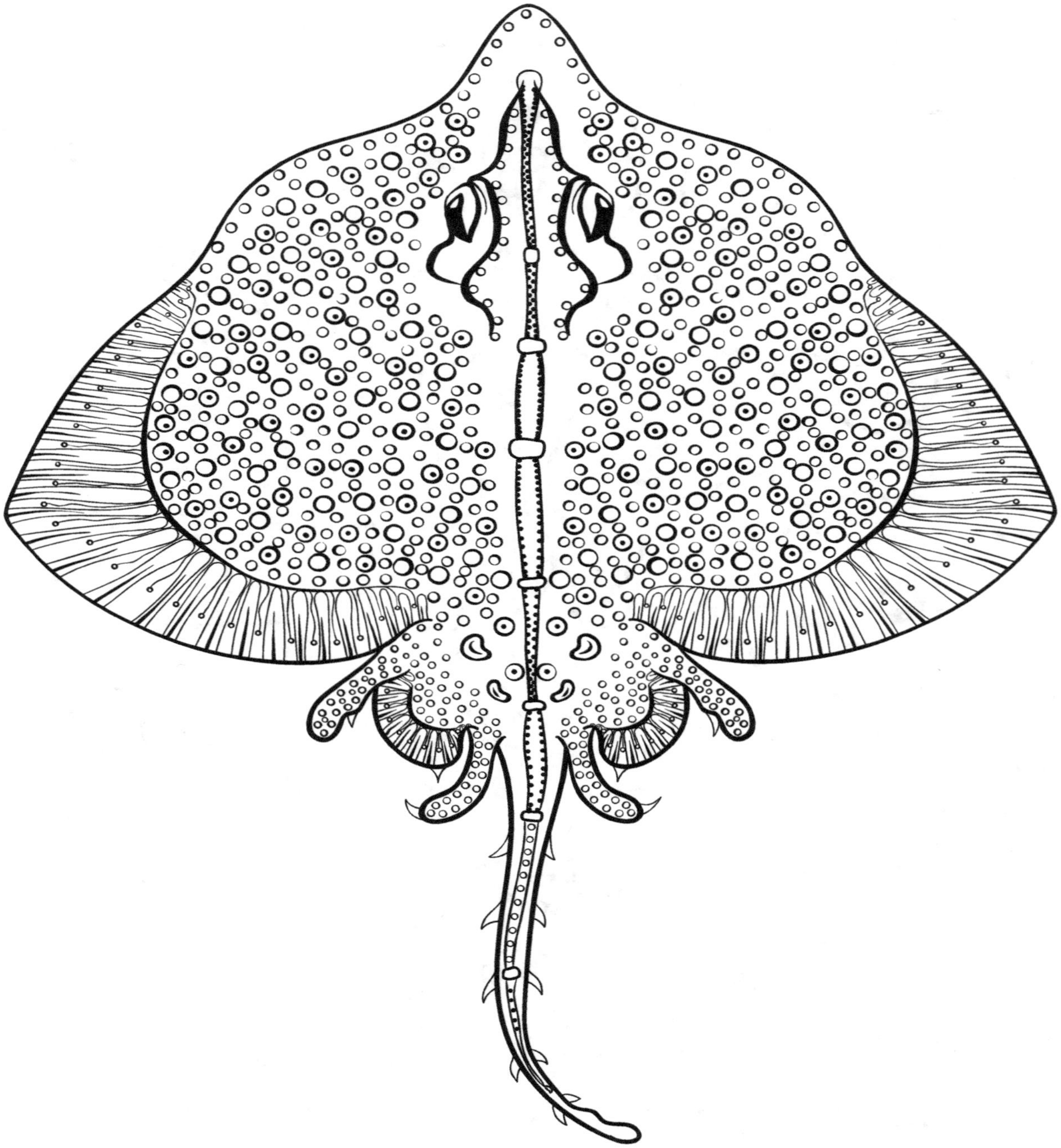

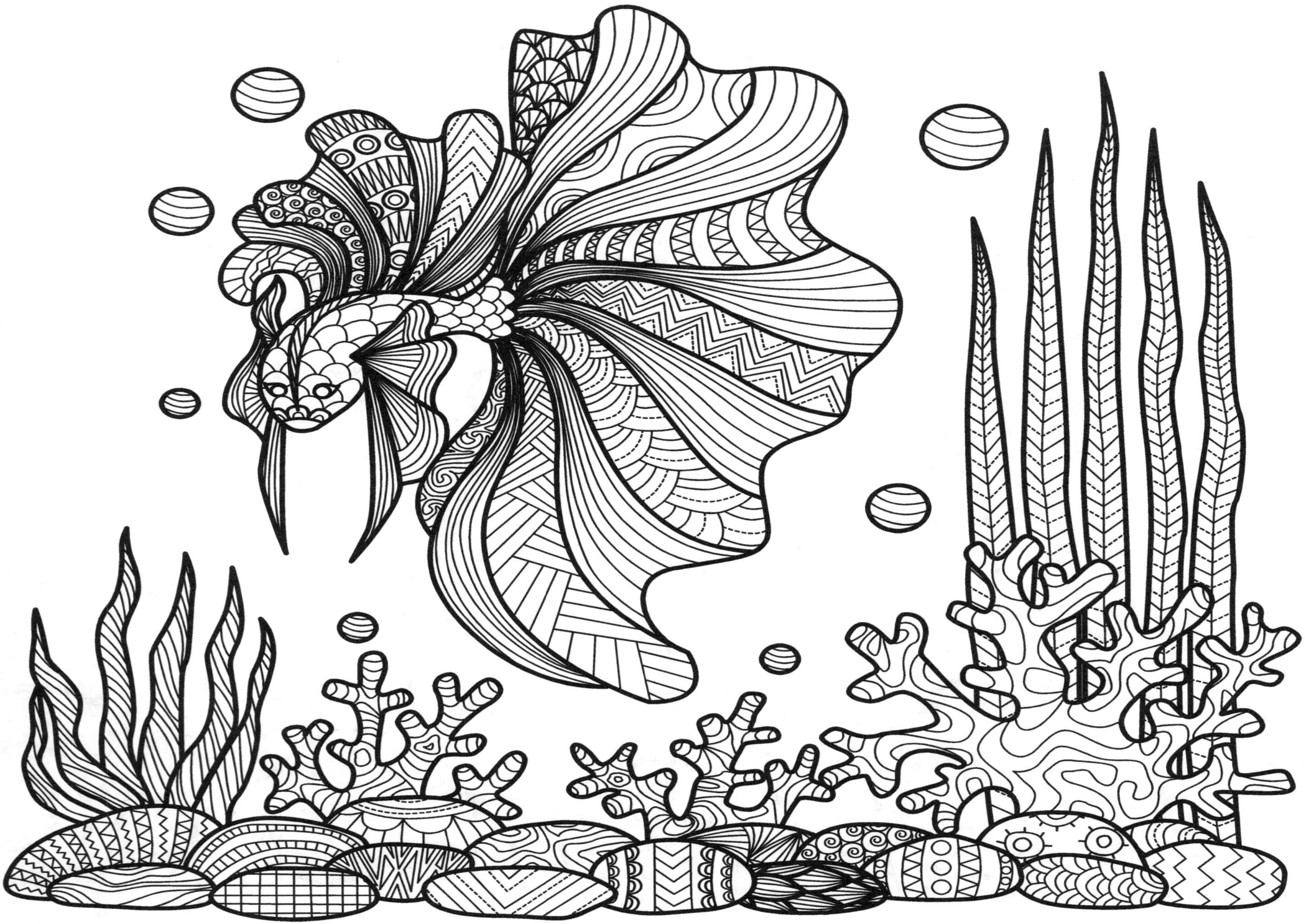

Adventure Learning Press
adventurelearningpress.com

www.ingramcontent.com/pod-product-compliance
Lightning Source LLC
Chambersburg PA
CBHW081542280526
45788CB00010B/3331
9781530791873